SEVEN WONDERS OF THE WORLD

SEVEN WONDERS OF THE MODERN WORLD

A MyReportLinks.com Book

Doreen Gonzales

MyReportLinks.com Books
an imprint of

Enslow Publishers, Inc.
Box 398, 40 Industrial Road
Berkeley Heights, NJ 07922
USA

MyReportLinks.com Books, an imprint of Enslow Publishers, Inc. MyReportLinks® is a registered trademark of Enslow Publishers, Inc.

Library of Congress Cataloging-in-Publication Data

Gonzales, Doreen.
    Seven wonders of the modern world / Doreen Gonzales.
        p. cm. — (Seven wonders of the world)
    Includes bibliographical references and index.
    ISBN 0-7660-5292-3
    1. Engineering—Juvenile literature. 2. Seven Wonders of the World—Juvenile literature. 3. Architecture—Juvenile literature. I. Title. II. Series.
    TA149.G64 2005
    620—dc22
                                2004015255

Printed in the United States of America

10 9 8 7 6 5 4 3 2 1

To Our Readers:
Through the purchase of this book, you and your library gain access to the Report Links that specifically back up this book.
The Publisher will provide access to the Report Links that back up this book and will keep these Report Links up to date on **www.myreportlinks.com** for five years from the book's first publication date.
We have done our best to make sure all Internet addresses in this book were active and appropriate when we went to press. However, the author and the Publisher have no control over, and assume no liability for, the material available on those Internet sites or on other Web sites they may link to.
The usage of the MyReportLinks.com Books Web site is subject to the terms and conditions stated on the Usage Policy Statement on **www.myreportlinks.com**.
A password may be required to access the Report Links that back up this book. The password is found on the bottom of page 4 of this book.
Any comments or suggestions can be sent by e-mail to comments@myreportlinks.com or to the address on the back cover.

Photo Credits: © 1996–2004 ACSE, p. 6; © 1997–2004 CN Tower, p. 29; © 1999 PhotoDisc, pp. 1, 18, 20, 23; © 2003 Toronto place.com, p. 31; © 2004 Eurotunnel plc, p. 40; © 2004 The Cornwallis School, Kent, UK, p. 36; © Corel Corporation, pp. 3, 9, 16, 27, 32, 38; © Energy.Saving.nu 2000, p. 34; Empire State Building Company, LLC, p. 22; Enslow Publishers, Inc., p. 7; History of the CN Tower, p. 30; MyReportLinks.com Books, p. 4; Panama Canal Authority, p. 12; PBS Online, pp. 25, 35; Smithsonian Institution Libraries, p. 11; Watchavision, p. 14.

Cover Photo: © 1999 PhotoDisc

Cover Description: The Golden Gate Bridge in San Francisco, California.

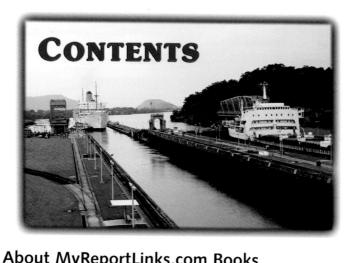

CONTENTS

About MyReportLinks.com Books 4

Seven Wonders of the Modern
   World Facts. 5

1 Humans Against Nature 6

2 The Panama Canal 9

3 North Sea Protection Works 14

4 The Empire State Building 18

5 The Golden Gate Bridge 23

6 CN Tower 27

7 The Itaipu Dam 32

8 The Channel Tunnel 36

Report Links 41

Glossary. 43

Chapter Notes 44

Further Reading 47

Index 48

MyReportLinks.com Books
Great Books, Great Links, Great for Research!

The Internet sites featured in this book can save you hours of research time. These Internet sites—we call them **"Report Links"**—are constantly changing, but we keep them up to date on our Web site.

When you see this "Approved Web Site" logo, you will know that we are directing you to a great Internet site that will help you with your research.

Give it a try! Type http://www.myreportlinks.com into your browser, click on the series title and enter the password, then click on the book title, and scroll down to the Report Links listed for this book.

The Report Links will bring you to great source documents, photographs, and illustrations. MyReportLinks.com Books save you time, feature Report Links that are kept up to date, and make report writing easier than ever! A complete listing of the Report Links can be found on pages 41–42 at the back of the book.

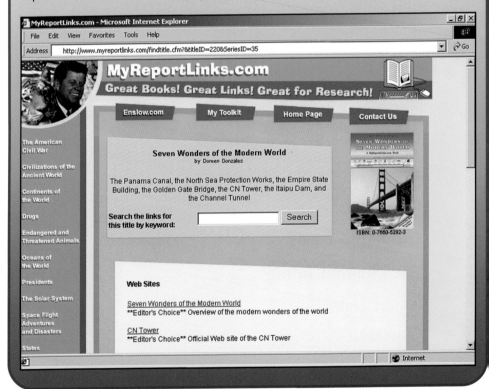

Please see "To Our Readers" on the copyright page for important information about this book, the MyReportLinks.com Web site, and the Report Links that back up this book.

Please enter **SWM1781** if asked for a password.

Seven Wonders of the Modern World Facts

The Panama Canal

* The Panama Canal stretches from Colón to Panama City, Panama.
* Construction took place from 1904 to 1914.
* The canal is roughly fifty miles (eighty-one kilometers) long.
* The cost of the Panama Canal was $352 million.

North Sea Protection Works

* The North Sea Protection Works are located in the Netherlands.
* They were built from 1923 to 1986.
* Oosterscheldedam is the longest of the works, covering 6 miles (9.7 kilometers).
* The cost to build was $5 billion.

The Empire State Building

* New York City, New York, is the home of the Empire State Building.
* The Empire State Building was built from 1929 to 1931.
* It is 1,250 feet (381 meters) in height.
* It cost just over $24.7 billion to build the Empire State Building. Including the price of the land, the total cost was over $40.9 billion.

The Golden Gate Bridge

* The Golden Gate Bridge is located in San Francisco, California, and spans a body of water known as the Golden Gate Strait.
* Building the Golden Gate Bridge lasted from 1933 to 1937.
* The bridge is 8,981 feet (2,737 meters) long.
* The cost of building the Golden Gate Bridge was $27 million.

CN Tower

* The CN Tower is located in Toronto, Canada.
* It was built from 1973 to 1975.
* The CN Tower stretches to 1,815 feet, 5 inches (553.3 meters).
* It cost 63 million Canadian dollars to build the CN Tower.

The Itaipu Dam

* The Itaipu Dam spans the Paraná River between the countries of Brazil and Paraguay.
* Construction on the dam took place from 1975 to 1991.
* The dam is about five miles (eight kilometers) long.
* It cost $18 billion to build the dam.

The Channel Tunnel

* The Channel Tunnel, known simply as the Chunnel, stretches underneath the English Channel from Folkestone, England, to Coquelles, France.
* Building the Chunnel began in 1987, and it was not opened until 1994.
* The Chunnel is 32 miles (51.5 kilometers) long, of which 23 miles (37 kilometers) is under the sea.
* Completion of the tunnel cost $21 billion.

Chapter 1 ▶

HUMANS AGAINST NATURE

Each of the structures in this book began as a dream to move faster, go higher, or live better. The Panama Canal, for example, was built to speed travel between the Pacific and Atlantic Oceans. Its construction required removing enough dirt and rubble to open a 16-foot (5-meter) wide tunnel to the center of the earth.[1] The Channel Tunnel, an undersea train tunnel that stretches

In 1994, the American Society of Civil Engineers chose the Seven Wonders of the Modern World. This book looks at each of the wonders on the list. This is part of the ASCE Web site **Seven Wonders of the Modern World.**

EDITOR'S CHOICE

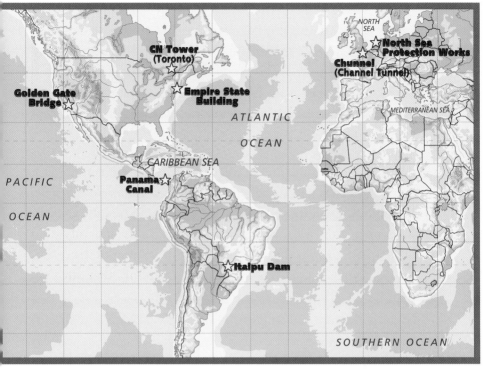

▲ *This world map shows where each of the modern wonders are located.*

from Britain to France, was also built to help people travel faster. The need for speed was considered in all aspects of this project. The trains that move through the tunnel have a locomotive on each end to hasten a train's exit in case of emergency.[2]

Some structures were built to go higher than ever before. the Empire State Building, for instance, was built because of a dream to construct the highest building in the world. It is so tall, there is over 17 million feet (5 million meters) of telephone wire inside it.[3] This is more than enough wire to stretch from New York City to Los Angeles, California.[4] The nearly two thousand feet tall CN Tower was also built to go as high as possible. For those not convinced of its spectacular height, a simulator inside features a virtual bungee jump from the top of the tower.[5]

The desire to live better is what motivated the construction of the North Sea Protection Works. These dams and barriers hold back the ocean and protect the people of the Netherlands from flooding. Its longest dam is the Oosterscheldedam. It is as long as one thousand school buses parked end to end.[6] Itaipu Dam in South America began as a vision to create electricity for the people of Paraguay and Brazil. The completed energy plant includes a dam so massive, it contains enough iron and steel to build three hundred Eiffel Towers.[7]

None of the structures in this book were easy to build. Each one pitted human ingenuity and perseverance against nature. In the end, human desire triumphed. Along the way, new machines were often invented and new engineering methods devised. For example, the engineers of the Golden Gate Bridge worked for months solving mathematical equations to create a bridge that could withstand 100 mile-per-hour (185.2 kilometer-per-hour) winds. Their work was done before the age of computers, with nothing more than slide rules and adding machines to crunch numbers. The result? A bridge that safely swings nearly twenty-eight feet (nine meters).[8]

As their creators imaginatively overcame obstacles, these structures became the marvels of their day. Each was so innovative, in fact, that the American Society of Civil Engineers named them the Seven Wonders of the Modern World. According to the organization, they are examples of modern society's ability to "achieve the unachievable, reach unreachable heights, and scorn the notion 'it can't be done.'"[9]

Chapter 2

THE PANAMA CANAL

The Panama Canal creates one of the longest shortcuts in the world. Before it was built, ships going from the Atlantic Ocean to the Pacific Ocean had to sail around South America. The new canal made it possible to cut through Panama, a country at the southern end of North America. This took about eight thousand miles (thirteen thousand kilometers) off the journey. It is such a useful route that thousands of cargo, military, and cruise ships travel through the canal each year.

▲ *The Panama Canal made it possible for people to sail from the Atlantic Ocean to the Pacific Ocean without having to go around the southern tip of the South American continent.*

The Need For a Canal

People had dreamed of connecting the oceans as far back as the 1500s. It would be centuries, though, before the proper machinery and know-how made a canal possible.

In the late 1800s, a canal seemed achievable. The French were the first to try. However, their machines were too small, and tropical diseases killed many workers. By the end of the century, they had given up.

The dream did not die, though. United States President Theodore Roosevelt saw how valuable a canal would be for moving goods and people. Furthermore, he was convinced a canal was essential to the defense of the United States. It would allow the American Navy's fleet of ships to move quickly from one side of the country to the other.

In 1903, the United States government paid Panama $10 million for the right to build and operate a canal there.[1] The first task was to make the area safe for workers. Crews cleared brush and drained swamps, killing millions of disease-carrying mosquitoes that had devastated the French attempt.

A Cut, A Lake, and Some Locks

Soon steam shovels were digging through the hills on the Pacific side of Panama. The earth here was very loose, and landslides slowed the work. It took several years to make a cut 8 miles (13 kilometers) long. During that time, tons of earth were removed to make a channel called the Gaillard Cut.

The earth taken from the Gaillard Cut was hauled by train to the other side of the country. There it was used to make a dam across the Chagres River. Once finished, the dam backed water into a valley to create Gatun Lake.

Gatun Lake and the Gaillard Cut would form the main waters of the Panama Canal. Yet both lay above ocean waters. Therefore, ships would have to be raised and lowered to use the canal. This required structures called locks.

The Bucyrus Co. of South Milwaukee, Wisconsin, manufactured most of the 102 steam shovels used to dig the canal. The largest weighed 95 tons (86 metric tons) with dippers capable of extracting up to five cubic yards (four cubic meters) in each cycle. Ten hours a day, six days a week, they loaded from 4,000 to 6,000 cubic yards (3,000 to 4,600 cubic meters) of stiff clay and blasted rock.

Even with this capacity, it took more than nine of nearly non-st create the nin (14.5-kilomet Cut, which c Lake and the Locks across continental divi

This dipper from a 70-ton steam shovel has a scooping volume of three cubic yards (2.3 cubic meters).

Workers operated 102 steam shovels, such as the one shown here, to dig the Panama Canal. This image can be found on the Smithsonian Institution's Web site called **Make the Dirt Fly!**

A lock is a giant tank used to move ships between two levels of water. A vessel moves into a lock, and the gates of the lock are closed. Water is poured into the chamber or drained out until the level inside the lock is the same as on the other side of the water that the ship is moving toward. Then the gate opens, and the ship sails out.

The locks of the Panama Canal were one of the biggest engineering challenges of the project. They were built in pairs to allow vessels to travel both ways on the canal at the same time. At 110 feet (34 meters) wide and 1,000 feet (305 meters) long, they were the largest concrete structures ever built.[2]

The steel gates for the locks were also massive. Each one weighed more than 700 tons (635 metric tons). They were opened and closed with a 40-horsepower engine.[3] This is the same size motor used to power a small boat.

The Cost of a Canal

During the busiest construction period, almost forty-five thousand people were working on the canal. Most came from the British West Indies, but many were from the United States.

The canal was completed in 1914 at a cost of $352 million.[4] Another kind of cost was the number of deaths. Over five thousand people died from injury or illness while working to complete the canal.[5]

Through the Canal

On August 15, 1914, the first ship, the SS *Ancon*, sailed through the Panama Canal. Its journey was much the same as the trip is today.

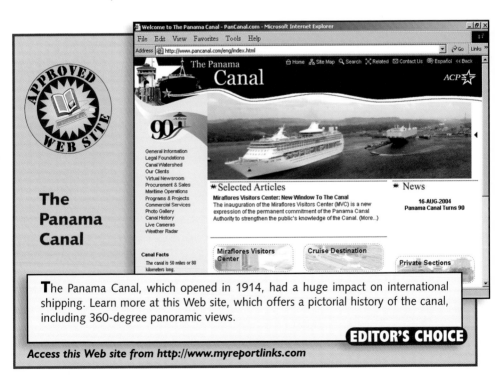

The Panama Canal, which opened in 1914, had a huge impact on international shipping. Learn more at this Web site, which offers a pictorial history of the canal, including 360-degree panoramic views.

EDITOR'S CHOICE

Access this Web site from http://www.myreportlinks.com

A vessel coming from the Atlantic Ocean is hooked to locomotives that guide it through the Gatun Locks. These locks raise the ship 85 feet (26 meters) to Gatun Lake.

After a 32-mile (51-kilometer) journey across the lake, the ship sails through the Gaillard Cut. At the end of the cut, it enters the Pedro Miguel Locks. These lower the ship 30 feet (9 meters) to another lake. From here it moves through the Miraflores Locks and is let down another 52 feet (16 meters) to the Pacific Ocean. The 50-mile (80-kilometer) trip takes about eight hours. The locks by the Pacific Ocean lower ships three feet more than the Atlantic Ocean locks. This is because the sea level here is three feet lower.

The Canal Today

In 1977, the United States agreed to gradually transfer ownership of the canal to Panama. The transition was complete at the end of 1999. Since then, Panama has improved the canal by widening the Gaillard Cut and improving the locks. With these changes, the hope is that the canal will be used for many years to come.

Chapter 3 ▶

NORTH SEA PROTECTION WORKS

People that live in the Netherlands are fond of saying, "God created the world, but the Dutch created Holland." The Netherlands, sometimes called Holland, is a country in Europe that borders the North Sea. Its people are known as the Dutch. Much of the Netherlands lies below sea level, making it easy to flood.

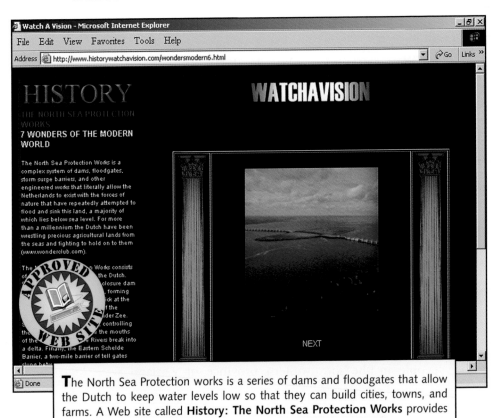

The North Sea Protection works is a series of dams and floodgates that allow the Dutch to keep water levels low so that they can build cities, towns, and farms. A Web site called **History: The North Sea Protection Works** provides online information and images about this major feat of engineering.

For centuries, the Dutch built dikes to hold back the sea. Sometimes they built dikes around shallow water, then emptied the area using windmill-powered pumps. The water was channeled back to the ocean through man-made canals. The newly drained land, called a polder, was used to live on. Farms, towns, and even large cities have been built on polders.

Yet dikes have not always held back the sea during severe storms. When a dike broke, water often washed away houses, farms, and people. Two devastating storms—one that occurred in 1916 and another in 1953—prompted the Dutch government to build new barriers along the sea. The resulting dams and floodgates are known as the North Sea Protection Works.

The Zuiderzeeworks

In 1916, a terrible storm killed hundreds of people around the Zuider Zee, a large inlet in the northern part of the Netherlands. The government immediately planned a protection project called the Zuiderzeeworks.

First, a 19-mile (31-kilometer) long dam was built across the Zuider Zee. The structure was made from clay, sand, stone, and "mattresses" of small trees and bushes. This dam was 25 feet (8 meters) high and as thick as a football field.[1] Some of the water inside the dam was drained, creating an area of polders that was called Flevoland. The remaining water became a freshwater lake named Ijsselmeer. This part of the North Sea Protection Works was finished in 1932.

When another huge storm blew across the North Sea in 1953, the Zuiderzeeworks held. However, nearly two thousand people in the southwestern province of Zeeland were killed by flooding waters. The Dutch government was determined to prevent another similar disaster and began a program called the Delta Plan.

Enkuizen (shown here) is one of the Dutch cities that would flood frequently if the North Sea Protection Works had not been built.

The Delta Plan

Zeeland is a land of peninsulas and islands interrupted by several deltas. A delta is a fan-shaped deposit of sand and soil that forms at the mouth of a river. Engineers decided the region needed several different kinds of barriers. So they planned various structures, not sure of how the larger ones would be built. But they felt confident that as the smaller structures were constructed, the technology and expertise for making the bigger pieces would develop.[2]

First, several dikes were heightened. Then three main dams were built across the estuaries of the Rhine, Mass, and Scheldt rivers (an estuary is the place where a river meets the sea). Channels were left open for ocean vessels to get to and from Rotterdam, the Netherlands, and Antwerp, Belgium. Then it was time to build the most complex part of the project—a surge barrier that would dam the Oosterschelde estuary.

The Oosterscheldedam

The Oosterscheldedam was planned as a closed barrier. However, fishermen and conservationists knew this would destroy much of the marine life inside the dam. They persuaded the government to build a barrier that would remain open most of the time, but be closed when bad weather threatened. This would minimize interference with the natural environment.

Sixty-five giant concrete piers were needed, each weighing around eighteen thousand tons (sixteen thousand metric tons) and standing as tall as a twelve-story building.[3] Two artificial islands were built in the Oosterschelde estuary for constructing the piers.

Once the piers were completed, specially made vessels towed them into the sea and strung them between the work islands and the mainland. Computers aboard the boats and on the shore guided the positioning of each. The technology was so precise, every one of the piers was placed within 4 inches (10 centimeters) of its planned position.[4] Then tons of sand and rock were piled along the bottom of the piers, anchoring them against the battering tides of the North Sea.

Next, huge steel gates were lowered between the piers. These gates could be closed by a control station on one of the work islands. The gates and mechanisms are so well engineered, the entire barrier can be closed in just one hour. The Oosterschelde storm surge barrier was finished in 1986.

▷ Living With the Sea

The final price tag of the Delta Plan alone was $5 billion.[5] To the Dutch, the safety is well worth the money.

In addition to providing safety to the people of Holland, the dams have created new recreation areas. Roadways have been built on top of some to improve transportation routes throughout the region. Finally, the larger dams are a tourist attraction. A museum near the Oostercheldedam describes how the dams were built.

The North Sea Protection Works has been called a wonder of the world because of its size and the technical expertise needed to create it. One professional magazine remarked, "It is unique, expensive, and quite unlike any other civil engineering project to be found on this planet."[6] It is proof that if the Dutch did not actually create Holland, they are certainly preserving it.

Chapter 4 ▶

THE EMPIRE STATE BUILDING

The movie audience gasped. What would King Kong do with the beautiful heroine, Fay Wray, when he got to the top of the skyscraper? Everyone watching the 1933 movie knew the gigantic ape was climbing the tallest building in the world, the Empire State Building. It was, and still is, one of the most famous structures ever built.

▲ *The Empire State Building is the centerpiece of midtown Manhattan. People can go up to the eighty-sixth-floor observation deck and look out over the surrounding area.*

The Empire State Building is located in New York City, and it was the world's tallest building from 1931 until 1972. Today, only a handful of buildings rise higher.

The Race to the Sky

During the late 1800s, builders began using steel to frame tall buildings. Steel frameworks made it possible to erect taller and taller structures. Soon the skyscraper was born, and each one seemed to go higher.

Before long, some people made a competition of erecting the world's tallest building. First came the Woolworth Building in 1913. It is 792 feet (241 meters) high. The Bank of Manhattan Trust topped this in 1930 at 927 feet (283 meters). The Chrysler Building was next, also in 1930. It is 1,046 feet (319 meters) tall.[1]

Yet even before the Chrysler Building was finished, investor John Jacob Raskob was making plans to go higher. He wanted to erect a building as a tribute to America's wealth of opportunity.[2] Raskob named his dream after New York state's nickname, and the Empire State Building began taking shape.

Designing the Building

New York City zoning laws said that tall buildings could not block sunlight from reaching the street. So the 1,250-foot (381-meter) building was designed to decrease in size as it grew taller, allowing sunshine to fall to the ground.

Mail chutes, toilets, and elevator shafts would be built in the center of each floor, with office space around the outside. This would allow every worker to be within 25 feet (8 meters) of a window.

The building also had to include enough elevators to move thousands of people among one hundred floors. The finished structure would boast seventy-three elevators. Finally, Raskob wanted the top of his building to have a docking station for dirigibles. At the time, these airships were used for transportation.

◁ *The lights that illuminate the top of the Empire State Building change colors at various times throughout the year. In this photo the lights are red and green to celebrate the Christmas season.*

▷ Building the World's Tallest Structure

By March 1930, the building site had been cleared, and the footings (the parts of the base that make sure the building is not tilted to one side) were set. Then, like giant pieces from an Erector toy construction set, exactly measured beams and girders were delivered for the building's frame. These beams and girders already had rivet holes drilled into them.

As steelworkers framed the building, other workers followed behind, pouring concrete for each story's floor. Next came more workers who installed the limestone blocks and windows of the exterior walls. Behind them, electricians, plumbers, and carpenters finished the interior spaces. At the height of construction, more than three thousand people were working on the building at once.[3]

In order to keep all of these workers busy, an immense amount of supplies had to be at the right place at the right time. A company was hired for the sole purpose of organizing and delivering materials.

This "assembly line" method was new to the construction industry. It was also fast. It took only seven months for workers to get to the eighty-sixth floor. Other builders noted this efficiency and were soon utilizing the same procedures.

Obstructions

There were some problems with the construction of the Empire State Building. One was the wind. The higher in the air, the stronger the wind's force. So engineers designed special ways of connecting the framework to improve the building's strength against the wind. These and other techniques made the building so solid, it was easily repaired when an airplane accidentally crashed into it in 1945. Even so, strong winds can still cause the building to sway.

The wind also caused problems with the dirigible dock. A 200-foot (61-meter) tower on top of the eighty-sixth floor was meant to be the mooring mast for dirigibles that would help the airships dock. Two airships tested the dock, and both could barely land due to high winds. So the plan was abandoned, and an observation deck was installed at the top of the tower instead. This was the equivalent of the 102nd story.

The worst setbacks of all were the accidents. Five people were killed during construction.[4] The emphasis on constructing the building quickly may have been the cause. Yet this did not slow the pace for long. The Empire State Building was finished fourteen months after site excavation began. The grand structure alone had cost $24,718,000 to build.[5] The entire project cost about 40.9 million dollars.

Finished

The Empire State Building opened with a ceremony that involved President Herbert Hoover. On May 1, 1931, he pressed a symbolic button in the White House to turn on its lights.

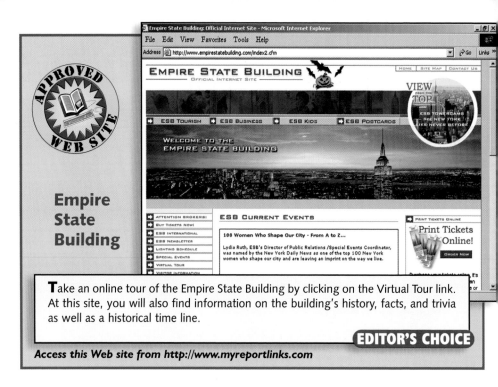

Empire
State
Building

Take an online tour of the Empire State Building by clicking on the Virtual Tour link. At this site, you will also find information on the building's history, facts, and trivia as well as a historical time line.

EDITOR'S CHOICE

Access this Web site from http://www.myreportlinks.com

Today, the building is filled with over ten thousand places of business, ranging from banks and offices to restaurants and jewelry stores. However there are no offices in the building's tower for safety reasons.

In addition, millions of tourists visit the eighty-sixth-floor observation deck each year. The 102nd-floor tower observation deck has been closed to the public, because officials feared it was not safe.

Raskob succeeded in building a tribute to his beloved country. The result was so spectacular, in fact, that even though the Empire State Building is no longer the tallest building in the world, it has become a symbol of America known around the globe.

THE GOLDEN GATE BRIDGE

Few people visit San Francisco, California, without seeing the Golden Gate Bridge. This splendid, bright orange structure spans the entrance to San Francisco Bay, connecting the city to northern California. The Golden Gate Bridge is 8,981 feet (2,737 meters) long.[1] It was the longest suspension bridge in the world for twenty-seven years after it was completed in 1937.

▶ We Need a Bridge

San Francisco sits at the end of a peninsula, separated from northern California by the Golden Gate Strait. A strait is a narrow

▲ The Golden Gate Bridge connects the city of San Francisco to Marin County, California. The bridge's orange paint makes it very recognizable.

body of water that joins two larger bodies of water. For many years the only way to cross the strait was by ferry.

During the 1920s, the ferries became more and more crowded, and people often waited for hours, and even days to cross. A bridge seemed like a logical solution, and a group began raising money for the project.

Other people thought the idea was foolish. They believed that the constant fog, high winds, earthquake problems, and strong ocean currents made a bridge impossible. They called it the "bridge that couldn't be built."[2]

Strauss's Certainty

Engineer Joseph Baerman Strauss disagreed. He designed a suspension bridge he felt could withstand all of these natural forces. His bridge would consist of two towers strung with thick metal cables that held up a six-lane road. It would need the tallest towers, the largest piers, and the longest and thickest cables ever built. Strauss was confident it could be done.[3]

Work on the Bridge Begins

Work on the bridge began in January 1933 when enormous concrete blocks were laid on either side of the strait and fastened to bedrock. The bridge's cables would be attached to beams and cemented into the blocks. These anchors would keep the weight of the bridge from bending the towers toward each other.

Meanwhile, concrete piers were being built to hold each tower. Strauss and other engineers designed the bridge so the two towers could be as close together as possible while still creating the needed span of 4,200 feet (1,280 meters). Therefore, the position of each pier was determined by engineering considerations rather than by the convenience of any particular site. This created problems.

The northern pier was situated in shallow water, and it went up easily. But the southern pier had to be built in deep ocean water. A special kind of dam had to be built before the pier could be constructed. This held ocean waters back so workers could complete construction of the pier. The San Francisco pier was finally finished in late 1935.

The Towers

Now the towers could be erected on the top of each pier. A crane hoisted land-built sections into place, then workers fastened them together. The finished towers stood 746 feet (227 meters) tall.

Suspension cables were then strung from the anchor on one side of the bridge, over the towers, and into the anchor on the other side. Each one was about 36 inches (91 centimeters) in diameter. The two cables contained 80,000 miles (128,720 kilometers) of steel wire, enough to circle the earth three times.[4]

The exact sag of the cables was carefully calculated. The cables had to be tight enough to support the road below the bridge. They also had to be loose enough to allow the bridge to move due

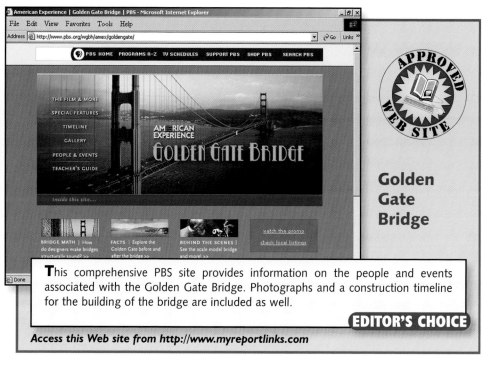

Golden Gate Bridge

This comprehensive PBS site provides information on the people and events associated with the Golden Gate Bridge. Photographs and a construction timeline for the building of the bridge are included as well.

EDITOR'S CHOICE

Access this Web site from http://www.myreportlinks.com

to stress or temperature changes. This flexibility would keep the structure from cracking during earthquakes, storms, or extreme weather changes.

Next, the cables for the road were hung from the suspension cables. They were each positioned to make the road 220 feet (67 meters) above the water so that United States Navy ships could pass under the bridge.

Building the Road

The road (U.S. Highway 101) was built in sections, starting at each of the towers and moving out in both directions at the same pace. This kept the strain on the towers and cables even. Sadly, ten men were killed while building the road. This brought the total number of deaths during the bridge's construction to eleven.[5]

Finally, it was time to pave the roadway deck and paint the bridge its unique international orange color. The bridge was finished in 1937, four years after it was begun. It had cost a total of $27 million.[6]

Success

On May 27, 1937, two hundred thousand people celebrated the opening of the Golden Gate Bridge by walking across it. The next day an official dedication ceremony was held, and the day after that, the bridge was opened to traffic.

Since then the "bridge that couldn't be built" has been used by millions of people. It has been closed due to bad weather only three times, and it survived a large earthquake in 1989. Today, engineers are working to make it even more earthquake-proof, ensuring that the Golden Gate Bridge will remain a San Francisco icon for years to come.

Chapter 6 ▶

CN TOWER

There are about sixty steps to the top of a three-story building. There are more than twenty-five hundred steps to the top of the CN Tower in Toronto, Canada.[1] At 1,815 feet, 5 inches (553.3 meters) high, it is the world's tallest tower.[2]

▷ A Tower for Power

During the late 1960s, Toronto became so crowded with tall buildings that television and radio signals were frequently disrupted. The Canadian National Railways Company (CN) decided to fix the problem by building a transmission tower that would stand far above Toronto's tallest buildings. As a tribute to Canadian industry, it was decided that this would be the tallest tower on earth.[3]

Engineers designed a concrete structure of three legs that fanned out in the shape of a 'Y.' Each leg

The CN Tower stands tall over ▷ the city of Toronto, Ontario, in Canada. It was built so that people living in the area could have clear television and radio reception.

would support an equal portion of the structure's 130,000-ton (118,014-metric ton) weight. The legs would narrow as they rose, making the tower taper like a gigantic needle pointing skyward.

A seven-story oval structure called the Sky Pod would be constructed about two thirds of the way up the tower. Then the tower would climb to an observation post called the Space Deck. Above it would be a broadcasting antenna.

Going Up

Work on the tower started in 1973 when more than sixty-two thousand tons of earth were dug from the site to get to the bedrock below. Here a 20-foot (6-meter) thick concrete foundation was poured.

Next, a huge mold was formed in the shape of the tower's legs. Concrete was poured into the mold that contained reinforcing cables and steel. Once it had set, hydraulic jacks pushed the mold upward, and it was filled again. The size of the mold decreased as it was raised, giving the tower its narrowing shape. Concrete was poured twenty-four hours a day, five days a week.

The Sky Pod

When the tower was 1,100 feet (335 meters) tall, it was ready for the Sky Pod. At its base was an area called the radome. This donut-shaped collar housed broadcasting equipment for the antenna. The radome was covered with a special Teflon-coated fabric that was only about as thick as a compact disk. Yet it was strong enough to protect the sensitive equipment from wind, weather, and even birds.

Visitor attractions were built above the radome. There is a revolving restaurant that gives diners a 360-degree view of Toronto and the sky. The Sky Pod also holds indoor and outdoor observation decks. One was later fitted with a glass floor, permitting viewers to gaze more than 1,000 feet (304.8 meters) straight down.

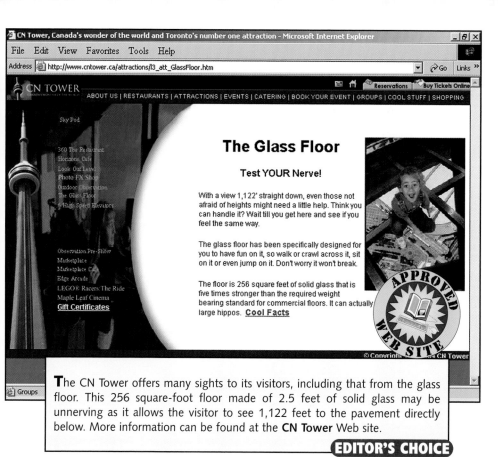

The CN Tower offers many sights to its visitors, including that from the glass floor. This 256 square-foot floor made of 2.5 feet of solid glass may be unnerving as it allows the visitor to see 1,122 feet to the pavement directly below. More information can be found at the **CN Tower** Web site.

EDITOR'S CHOICE

▷ *Olga*

After building the Sky Pod, more concrete was poured to build the tower upward another 200 feet (61 meters) to where the Space Deck would be constructed. At that point, the tower was ready for the broadcasting antennae. A Sikorsky Skycrane helicopter was used to install the 335-foot (102-meter) mast. However its first job was dismantling the crane that had been used to build the tower.

This almost ended in disaster. On the helicopter's first trip, the crane lurched as it was being hooked to the helicopter. This twisted the bolts that held the crane to the tower so that it could not be released. But the helicopter could not let go of the crane because there was an operator inside. The helicopter was stuck hovering over the tower with only a small amount of fuel. As time ran out, workers rushed to burn off the twisted bolts. Finally, the crane broke free with only minutes to spare.[4]

The near tragedy and heroic efforts of many rallied public interest in the project. The helicopter was soon nicknamed *Olga,* and newspapers, radio, and television stations began giving daily updates on her progress. During the next weeks, *Olga* lifted forty-four 7-ton (6-metric ton) antennae sections to the top of the tower where workers bolted them into place.

Completion

The CN Tower was completed in April 1975 at a cost of 63 million Canadian dollars.[5] It promptly took its place in the record books as the world's tallest tower. It is twice as tall as the Eiffel Tower and three times the height of the Space Needle in Seattle,

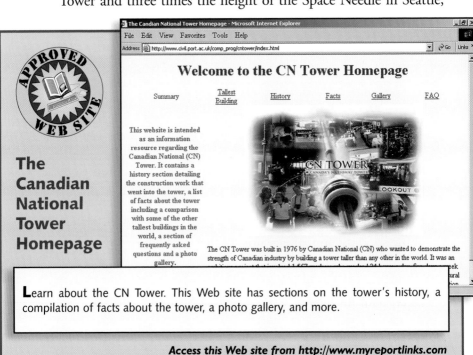

The Canadian National Tower Homepage

Learn about the CN Tower. This Web site has sections on the tower's history, a compilation of facts about the tower, a photo gallery, and more.

Access this Web site from http://www.myreportlinks.com

CN Tower:
Toronto
Place
Canada

This site from Toronto Place Canada provides a range of facts on the CN Tower in Toronto, Canada, including statistics on its height, location, cost, and weight.

Access this Web site from http://www.myreportlinks.com

Washington. Due to excellent engineering and precision building, it is off center by only 1.1 inches (3 centimeters).[6]

In addition to its claim to fame for height, the CN Tower dramatically improved broadcast signals in the area. Today, sixteen television and radio stations use the tower's equipment.

Toronto's Mascot

Each year 2 million tourists visit the CN Tower. Many take one of the six glass-fronted elevators to the Sky Pod. At the end of the 58-second ride is a 75-mile (121-kilometer) long view.

Just as impressive is looking up at the tower from the ground. Its graceful lines have come to define Toronto's skyline, making the CN Tower one of Canada's most famous attractions.

Chapter 7

THE ITAIPU DAM

It is hard to imagine a hydroelectric dam large enough to supply all the electric power needed to energize an entire country. Yet that is exactly what Itaipu Dam does. Located in South America between Brazil and Paraguay, Itaipu supplies nearly all of Paraguay's electricity and about one fourth of Brazil's.[1] It is, in fact, the largest renewable power plant in the world.[2]

▲ The Itaipu Dam was built on the Paraná River, bordering the nations of Brazil and Paraguay.

A Cooperative Effort

In 1973, Brazil and Paraguay decided to work together to build a hydroelectric dam on the Paraná River. The Paraná, the seventh largest river in the world, runs for several miles along the border that these two countries share. The dam site was chosen at a place called Itaipu.

In 1975, earth-moving machines were used to dig a channel that would change the course of the river. This exposed the riverbed so the dam could be constructed. Diverting the river involved moving millions of tons of earth and rock and took almost three years.

Once the space was ready, five different dams were built. The main dam was in the center. It was as high as a sixty-five-story building.[3] Two buttress dams were built on either side of it, and each of these was flanked by an embankment dam. Together, the structure was about five miles (eight kilometers) long.[4] When the five dams were completed in October 1982, the diversion channel was blocked, and water began rising behind the dam. Then, crews went out in boats to collect animals endangered by the rising water.[5]

Eventually, the released river created a reservoir over 14,000 square miles (36,260 square kilometers) in size. This is larger than the combined size of Massachusetts and Connecticut.

The Powerhouse

In an effort to stop water from the Paraná from flowing over the dam, eighteen enormous concrete pipes called penstocks were lined up vertically against the 5-mile (8-kilometer) dam. At the bottom of each penstock was a turbine and a generator. These eighteen generators formed the powerhouse that would create the electricity.

Each penstock would channel water from the reservoir to the powerhouse. The flowing water would spin the turbines, driving the generators to create electricity.

The first generators were ready to begin work in May 1984. Two or three more went into operation each year after that. By March 1991, the last generator was up and running.

Delivering Electricity

As the dam and powerhouse were being built, a system of transmission lines was constructed from Itaipu to cities in Paraguay and Brazil. These would create a power grid to carry the electricity from the plant to the people.

The many components of the dam called for a massive labor force. At the height of construction, thirty thousand people were working on the project. The total cost of Itaipu was $18 billion.[6]

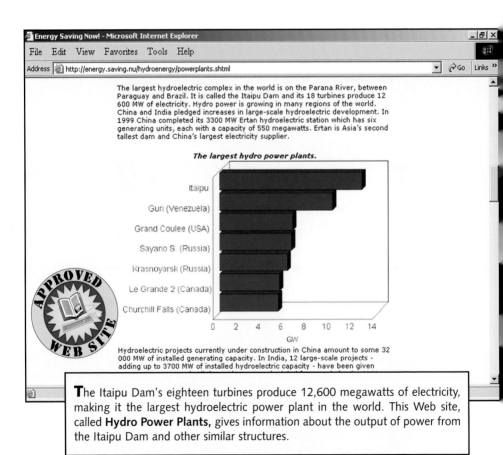

The Itaipu Dam's eighteen turbines produce 12,600 megawatts of electricity, making it the largest hydroelectric power plant in the world. This Web site, called **Hydro Power Plants,** gives information about the output of power from the Itaipu Dam and other similar structures.

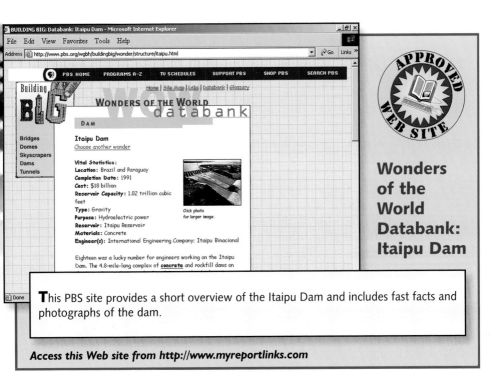

This PBS site provides a short overview of the Itaipu Dam and includes fast facts and photographs of the dam.

Access this Web site from http://www.myreportlinks.com

▷ Itaipu's Success

The Itaipu dam has been an overwhelming success. Its energy production has broken records, and in 2000 the dam produced a record 93.4 million megawatt-hours of energy.[7] This is enough to supply all of California.[8] Plus, Itaipu emits no pollutants.

Itaipu was an immense engineering feat. It is said that if the technical drawings for the project were stacked up, they would rise to the height of a fifty-story building.[9] Perhaps even more significant, though, is Itaipu's testament to how cooperation between nations can benefit all.

THE CHANNEL TUNNEL

Traveling in a train under the floor of the sea seems like something from a science fiction movie. Yet the Channel Tunnel is a reality. It connects France to England and is often referred to as the Chunnel.

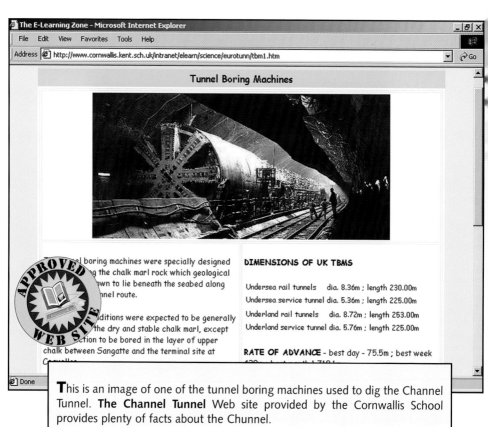

The E-Learning Zone - Microsoft Internet Explorer

File　Edit　View　Favorites　Tools　Help

Address http://www.cornwallis.kent.sch.uk/intranet/elearn/science/eurotunn/tbm1.htm

Tunnel Boring Machines

...l boring machines were specially designed ...g the chalk marl rock which geological ...wn to lie beneath the seabed along ...nnel route.

...ditions were expected to be generally ...the dry and stable chalk marl, except ...tion to be bored in the layer of upper chalk between Sangatte and the terminal site at C...........

DIMENSIONS OF UK TBMS

Undersea rail tunnels　dia. 8.36m ; length 230.00m
Undersea service tunnel dia. 5.36m ; length 225.00m
Underland rail tunnels　dia. 8.72m ; length 253.00m
Underland service tunnel dia. 5.76m ; length 225.00m

RATE OF ADVANCE - best day - 75.5m ; best week

Done

This is an image of one of the tunnel boring machines used to dig the Channel Tunnel. **The Channel Tunnel** Web site provided by the Cornwallis School provides plenty of facts about the Chunnel.

An Easier Way to Travel

Britain is separated from Europe's mainland by a strip of water called the English Channel. For centuries, the only way to cross the channel was by boat or air. Both were time-consuming and often uncomfortable.

Several solutions had been proposed over the years, including a tunnel, bridge, and combination of both. But the expertise for any project was not available until the 1980s. Then, engineers believed a tunnel through the soft rock at the bottom of the channel was possible.

Designing the Channel Tunnel

Knowing that an automobile tunnel would present too many ventilation problems, engineers proposed a tunnel for trains that could carry motor vehicles. These trains would be 14 feet (4 meters) across—the widest ever built.[1]

The resulting design was of three tunnels that ran parallel to each other. One was for trains going from Britain to France and another for trains moving from France to Britain. The third tunnel was for maintenance and emergency vehicles. It would run between the two.

Sonar and borings helped engineers determine the best route for the tunnel. It would cross the channel at one of its narrowest places, the Strait of Dover. The tunnel would begin at Folkestone, England. There it would dive underground for 32 miles (51.5 kilometers) to emerge at Coquelles, France. Twenty-three miles (37 kilometers) of the tunnel would run 150 feet (46 meters) under the bed of the sea.[2]

Tunneling Through the Earth

Building began in 1987 when shafts were dug into the earth on each side of the channel. Then specially designed tunnel boring machines (TBMs) were lowered into the shafts. Each TBM was as long as two football fields.[3] Their cutting heads were 30 feet (9 meters) in diameter.

As each machine cut its way through rock, one driver and a computerized laser guidance system kept it on course. The resulting debris was moved out by a conveyor belt, then taken back to the appropriate shaft.

On the British side of the channel, the material was dumped into an artificial lagoon created by a huge seawall. The water eventually evaporated, and a new piece of England was created. On the French side of the channel, the debris was dumped into a lake near the coast. Once filled, it was planted with grass.

As each TBM moved forward, machinery at the back lined the tunnel walls with pieces of pre-shaped concrete. These were later reinforced to make each tunnel wall 5 feet (2 meters) thick.[4]

△ This Eurostar is one of the trains that is used to transport people from Great Britain to France by way of the Chunnel.

When the tunnels were 300 feet (91 meters) apart, the TBMs were stopped. The remaining distance between the tunnels would be drilled with smaller machines so that the two ends could be perfectly aligned. Then the two tunnels would become one.

The TBMs had no reverse gear, and they could not be backed out of the tunnels. So when their job was finished, the machines on the English side were aimed downward and each burrowed itself into the bottom of the sea. The machines were dismantled except for the cutting heads, which were too difficult and expensive to remove. Instead, the cutting heads were left in the seabed and the holes were filled with concrete. Once the tunnels were joined, the French TBMs drove through the English side where they were pulled out of the shaft.

Tracks, Pipes, and Wires

Next, workers laid the railroad tracks. Then came the piping and pumping equipment that would carry cold water through the tunnel. The cold water is needed to cool down the heat caused by the friction of the trains.

Electricians wired security systems, signaling, and lighting. Workers built crossover tracks between the two tunnels. This way trains could continue running even when one of the tunnels had to be shut down.

The Channel Tunnel was finished at the end of 1993. On May 6, 1994, it opened with a ceremony attended by Queen Elizabeth II of Britain and French President François Mitterrand. Cost estimates vary for the project. The highest is $21 billion, making the Chunnel the most expensive civil engineering project in history.[5]

The Chunnel in the Twenty-First Century

Since opening, the Channel Tunnel has become a popular way to travel. People drive their cars onto a train at one end of the tunnel, then sit in the car while the train carries them to the other

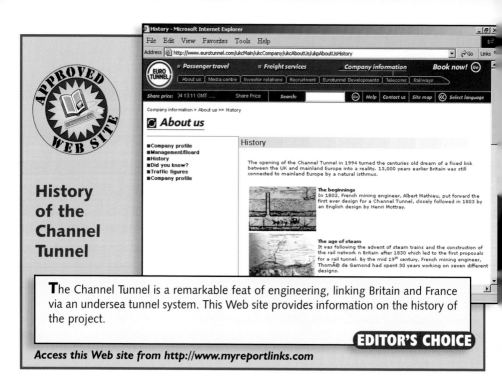

History of the Channel Tunnel

The Channel Tunnel is a remarkable feat of engineering, linking Britain and France via an undersea tunnel system. This Web site provides information on the history of the project.

EDITOR'S CHOICE

Access this Web site from http://www.myreportlinks.com

side. Moving at 100 miles per hour (161 kilometers per hour), this takes only thirty-five minutes, replacing a ninety-minute ferry ride.

Furthermore, some trains offer passenger service from London to Paris or Brussels. This takes about three hours. A high-speed rail link on the English side is currently being extended all the way to London.

In its first five years of operation, 28 million passengers and 12 million tons (10.9 metric tons) of freight moved through the Channel Tunnel.[6] To many Europeans and tourists, it is a fantastic new transportation system. To engineers, it is a marvel.

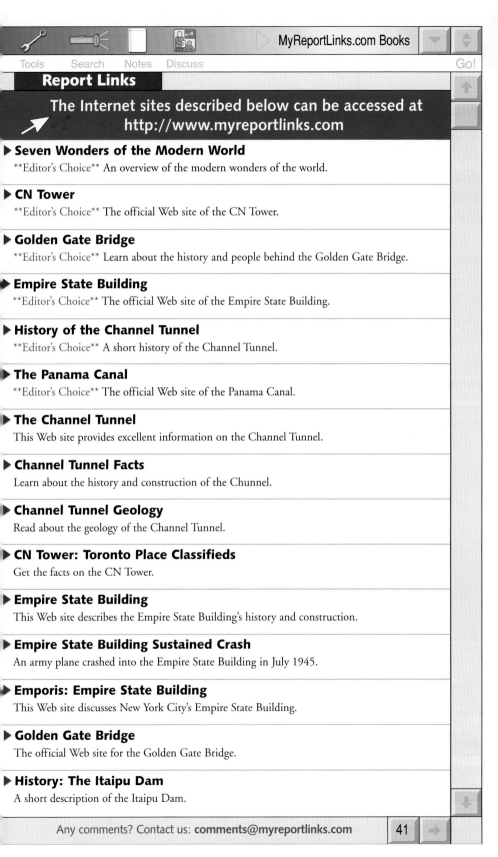
Report Links

The Internet sites described below can be accessed at http://www.myreportlinks.com

▶ **Seven Wonders of the Modern World**

Editor's Choice An overview of the modern wonders of the world.

▶ **CN Tower**

Editor's Choice The official Web site of the CN Tower.

▶ **Golden Gate Bridge**

Editor's Choice Learn about the history and people behind the Golden Gate Bridge.

▶ **Empire State Building**

Editor's Choice The official Web site of the Empire State Building.

▶ **History of the Channel Tunnel**

Editor's Choice A short history of the Channel Tunnel.

▶ **The Panama Canal**

Editor's Choice The official Web site of the Panama Canal.

▶ **The Channel Tunnel**

This Web site provides excellent information on the Channel Tunnel.

▶ **Channel Tunnel Facts**

Learn about the history and construction of the Chunnel.

▶ **Channel Tunnel Geology**

Read about the geology of the Channel Tunnel.

▶ **CN Tower: Toronto Place Classifieds**

Get the facts on the CN Tower.

▶ **Empire State Building**

This Web site describes the Empire State Building's history and construction.

▶ **Empire State Building Sustained Crash**

An army plane crashed into the Empire State Building in July 1945.

▶ **Emporis: Empire State Building**

This Web site discusses New York City's Empire State Building.

▶ **Golden Gate Bridge**

The official Web site for the Golden Gate Bridge.

▶ **History: The Itaipu Dam**

A short description of the Itaipu Dam.

Report Links

The Internet sites described below can be accessed at http://www.myreportlinks.com

▶ **History: The North Sea Protection Works**
An overview of the Dutch dike system.

▶ **History of the Tower**
Learn about the history and view pictures of the CN Tower.

▶ **Hydro Power Plants**
Read about hydroelectricity and the Itaipu Dam.

▶ **Itaipu Dam**
Learn about the Itaipu Hydroelectric Power Plant.

▶ **Itaipu Dam: Kent NGFL**
An overview of the Itaipu Dam with many facts and photos.

▶ **Make the Dirt Fly!**
This Smithsonian Web site discusses the construction of the Panama Canal.

▶ **The North Sea Protection Works**
Learn about the history of the North Sea Protection Works.

▶ **Panama: A Country Study**
The Library of Congress profiles the country of Panama.

▶ **The Panama Canal**
Learn about the Panama Canal through data, maps, and sketches.

▶ **Panama Canal Handover**
CNN describes the handover of the Panama Canal to Panama in 1999.

▶ **Panama Canal History Museum**
View historical photos and documents related to the Panama Canal.

▶ **theotherside.co.uk: Channel Tunnel**
The history of the Channel Tunnel is discussed at this Web site.

▶ **Today in History: The Empire State Building**
Read this Library of Congress article on the Empire State Building.

▶ **Wonders of the Modern World: The North Sea Protection Works**
This Web site provides the facts on the North Sea Protection Works.

▶ **Wonders of the World Databank: Itaipu Dam**
This PBS site gives a short overview of the Itaipu Dam.

Glossary

bedrock—The solid rock that lies beneath loose material such as soil.

boring machine—A machine that is used to dig cylinder-shaped tunnels in the ground.

canal—A long and narrow man-made waterway meant for boats to pass through or to provide water used for irrigation.

channel—A deep, narrow body of water separating two close land-masses.

delta—A fan-shaped deposit of sand and soil that forms at the mouth of a river.

dirigible—An airship such as a blimp.

estuary—The region at the mouth of a river where the river's fresh-water mixes with the saltwater from a sea.

ferry—A small vessel that moves people or vehicles across a body of water and departs and returns on a consistent schedule.

girder—A horizontal support beam that supports vertical beams used to construct a building.

hydroelectricity—Electricity created by water-powered turbine generators.

inlet—A narrow passage of water leading to a bay or lagoon.

straight—A narrow body of water that joins two larger bodies of water.

turbine—A machine containing rotating blades that are turned by flowing water.

ventilation—The process of circulating air so that contaminated air is replaced with fresh air.

Chapter 1. Humans Against Nature

1. American Society of Civil Engineers, "Seven Wonders of the Modern World," 1996–2004, <http://www.asce.org/history/seven_wonders.cfm#neder> (November 4, 2004).

2. Cathy Newman, "The Light at the End of the Chunnel," *National Geographic,* May 1994, p. 44.

3. "The Empire State Building," *WonderClub.com,* n.d., <http://wonderclub.com/WorldWonders/EmpireHistory.html> (October 18, 2004).

4. "Empire State Building Trivia and Cool Facts," *20th Century History,* n.d., <http://history1900s.about.com/library/misc/blempirefacts.htm> (October 18, 2004).

5. "Toronto—View From the CN Tower," *Kasbah.com,* 1997–2004, <http://www.kasbah.com/highlights/canada_toronto_view_from_the_cn_tower.htm> (October 18, 2004).

6. "Oosterschelde," *4Reference,* n.d., <http://www.4reference.net/encyclopedias/wikipedia/Oosterschelde.html> (October 18, 2004).

7. American Society of Civil Engineers, "Seven Wonders of the Modern World."

8. Golden Gate Bridge: Research Library, "Bridge Design and Construction Statistics," 2004, <http://www.goldengatebridge.org/research/factsGGBDesign.html?version=test#Bridgestats> (November 3, 2004).

9. American Society of Civil Engineers, "Seven Wonders of the Modern World."

Chapter 2. The Panama Canal

1. Panama Canal History, "American Canal Construction," 2001, <http://www.pancanal.com/eng/history/history/american.html> (November 4, 2004).

2. Neil Parkyn, ed., *The Seventy Wonders of the Modern World* (London: Thames and Hudson Ltd, 2002), p. 262.

3. Bob Cullen, "A Man, A Plan, A Canal: Panama Rises," *Smithsonian,* March 2004, p. 47.

4. Panama Canal History Museum, "canalmuseum.com," 2002, <http://www.canalmuseum.com/> (November 4, 2004).

5. Cullen, p. 47.

Chapter 3. North Sea Protection Works

1. National Geographic Society, as reprinted by *WonderClub.com,* "The North Sea Protection Works," n.d., <http://wonderclub.com/WorldWonders/ProtectionHistory.html> (November 4, 2004).

2. Kees d'Angremond, "From Disaster to Delta Project: The Storm Flood of 1953," *Terra et Aqua,* March 2003, <http://www.iadc-dredging.com/downloads/terra/terra-et-aqua_nr90_01.pdf> (November 4, 2004).

3. Larry Kohl, "The Oosterschelde Barrier: Man Against the Sea," *National Geographic,* October 1986, p. 532.

4. Ibid., p. 534.

5. Ibid., p. 527.

6. National Geographic Society, as reprinted at *WonderClub.com,* "The North Sea Protection Works."

Chapter 4. The Empire State Building

1. "Landmarks in American Civil Engineering History: Empire State Building," Civil Engineering, November/December 2002, p. 125.

2. Jeff Glasser, "Race to the Sky," *U.S. News and World Report,* June 30, 2003, p. 50.

3. Ibid., p. 53.

4. The History Net: 20th Century History, "Empire State Building Trivia and Cool Facts," 2004, <http://history1900s.about.com/library/misc/blempirefacts.htm> (November 3, 2004).

5. Ibid., p. 1.

Chapter 5. The Golden Gate Bridge

1. Golden Gate Bridge: Research Library, "Bridge Design and Construction Statistics," 2004, <http://www.goldengatebridge.org/research/factsGGBDesign.html?version=test#Bridgestats> (November 3, 2004).

2. John Bernard McGloin, "Symphonies in Steel: Bay Bridge and the Golden Gate," *Museum of the City of San Francisco,* n.d., <http://www.sfmuseum.net/hist9/mcgloin.html> (November 4, 2004).

3. Ibid., p. 4.

4. Golden Gate Bridge: Research Library, "Bridge Design and Construction Statistics."

5. Golden Gate Bridge: Research Library, "Frequently Asked Questions About the Golden Gate Bridge," 2004, <http://www.goldengatebridge.org/research/facts.html> (November 4, 2004).

6. Neil Parkyn, ed., *The Seventy Wonders of the Modern World* (London: Thames and Hudson Ltd., 2002), p. 235.

Chapter 6. CN Tower

1. National Geographic Society as reprinted by *WonderClub.com,* "The CN Tower," n.d., <http://wonderclub.com/WorldWonders/CNTowerHistory.html> (November 4, 2004).

2. American Society of Civil Engineers, "Seven Wonders of the Modern World," 1996–2004, <http://www.asce.org/history/seven_wonders.cfm#neder> (November 4, 2004).

3. CN Tower, "Cool Stuff: FAQ" *The CN Tower* <http://www.cntower.ca/faqs/l3_faq_faq_tower.htm> (November 4, 2004).

4. Ibid.

5. Neil Parkyn, ed., *The Seventy Wonders of the Modern World* (London: Thames and Hudson Ltd., 2002), p. 196.

6. American Society of Civil Engineers, "Seven Wonders of the Modern World."

Chapter 7. The Itaipu Dam

1. Itaipu Binancional—The World's Largest Power Plant, "Production," n.d., <http://www.itaipu.gov.br/english/dados/produ.htm> (November 4, 2004).

2. Itaipu Binancional—The World's Largest Power Plant, "Historical Background," n.d., <http://www.itaipu.gov.br/english/empre/histo.htm> (November 4, 2004).

3. American Society of Civil Engineers, "Seven Wonders of the Modern World," 1996–2004, <http://www.asce.org/history/seven_wonders.cfm#neder> (November 4, 2004).

4. Neil Parkyn, ed., *The Seventy Wonders of the Modern World* (London: Thames and Hudson Ltd., 2002), p. 267.

5. Ibid., p. 269.

6. Ibid., p. 267.

7. Itaipu Binancional—The World's Largest Power Plant, "Production."

8. Gregory T. Pope, "The Seven Wonders of the Modern World," *Popular Mechanics,* December 1995, p. 50.

9. "The Powerhouse," *The Geographical Magazine,* April 1996, p. 13.

Chapter 8. The Channel Tunnel

1. Gregory T. Pope, "The Seven Wonders of the Modern World," *Popular Mechanics,* December 1995, p. 52.

2. Neil Parkyn, ed., *The Seventy Wonders of the Modern World* (London: Thames and Hudson Ltd., 2002), p. 242.

3. Cathy Newman, "The Light at the End of the Chunnel," *National Geographic,* May 1994, p. 40.

4. Pope, p. 52.

5. PBS Online, "Channel Tunnel," *Building Big: Wonders of the World Data Bank,* 2000–2001, <http://www.pbs.org/wgbh/buildingbig/wonder/structure/channel.html> (November 4, 2004).

6. Ibid., p. 2.

Further Reading

Ash, Russell. *Great Wonders of the World.* New York: Dorling Kindersley, 2000.

Barter, James E. *The Golden Gate Bridge.* Farmington Hills, Mich.: Gale Group, 2001.

Cox, Rex, and Neil Morris. *The Modern World.* Philadelphia: Chelsea House Publishers, 2000.

Doherty, Craig A. and Katherine M. Doherty. *The Empire State Building.* Woodbridge, Conn.: Blackbirch Press, 1998.

Donovan, Sandy. *The Channel Tunnel.* Minneapolis: Lerner Publications, 2003.

Fine, Jil. *The Chunnel: The Building of a 200-Year Dream.* New York: Children's Press, 2003.

Greene, Meg. *The CN Tower.* San Diego, Calif.: Blackbirch Press, 2005.

Ingram, Scott. *The Panama Canal.* San Diego, Calif.: Blackbirch Press, 2004.

Mann, Elizabeth. *The Panama Canal.* New York: Mikaya Press, 1998.

———. *Empire State Building.* New York: Mikaya Press, 2003.

McDermott, Barb and Gail McKeown. *The CN Tower.* Edmonton: Reidmore Books, 1999.

Nelson, Sharlene and Ted. *The Golden Gate Bridge.* New York: Children's Press, 2001.

Simson, David. *The Netherlands.* Chicago: Raintree, 2004.

Thomas, Mark. *The Itaipu Dam: World's Biggest Dam.* New York: PowerKids Press, 2002.

Index

A
American Society of Civil Engineers, 6–7
assembly line, 21
C
Canadian National Railways, 27
Channel Tunnel
    commute, 40
    construction, 37–38
    design, 37
    location, 36–37
    nickname, 36
    tourism, 40
CN Tower
    construction, 28–30
    cost, 30
    design, 28
    height, 27, 30–31
    location, 27
    tourism, 31
D
Delta Plan, 15–16
E
Empire State Building
    construction, 20–21
    cost, 21
    design, 19
    location, 18–19
    problems, 21
    telephone wire, 8
    tourism, 22
Eurostar, 38
G
Gaillard Cut, 10, 13
Gatun Lake, 10, 13
Golden Gate Bridge
    construction, 24–26
    deaths, 26
    history, 23–24
    length, 23
    location, 23
    swing, 8
    tourism, 23
H
Hoover, Herbert, 21

I
international orange, 26
Itaipu Dam
    construction, 8, 33–34
    cost, 34
    hydroelectricity, 32–35
    location, 32–33
K
King Kong, 18
M
Miraflores Locks, 13
Mitterrand, François, 39
N
North Sea Protection Works
    construction, 15–17
    cost, 17
    history, 15
    location, 14
O
Olga, 29–30
Oosterscheldedam, 8, 16–17
P
Panama Canal
    construction, 7, 10–12
    cost, 12
    deaths, 12
    location, 9
    ownership, 10, 13
    shortcut, 9, 12–13
Paraná River, 32–33
Pedro Miguel Locks, 13
R
Raskob, John Jacob, 19, 22
Roosevelt, Theodore, 10
S
San Francisco Bay, 23
Sky Pod, 28–29, 31
SS *Ancon,* 12
Strauss, Joseph Baerman, 24
T
Tunnel boring machines, 36–39
U
United States Navy, 10, 26
Z
Zuiderzeeworks, 15

DATE DUE			

High Meadows School
Library Media Center
1055 Willeo Road
Roswell, GA 30075